Hebridean Solace

MY QUARTER-CENTURY LIVING WITH CANCER

MAIRI MACBRIDE

MCGEARY MEDIA

Foreword

Mairi MacBride ('Bunty') was originally named Mary MacBride. She was born on April 20th 1900 at 9 Camphill, Paisley, and died on February 20th 1980 at her home in Salen, Mull, where she lived most of her life. From 1940 to 1960 she worked as a teacher of dress design at the Burslem School of Art in the Staffordshire Potteries. There, she was in close contact with the Wedgwood designers, who worked nearby. She knew the factory's main man—Josiah Wedgwood. She also judged some of the new designs, and invited Wedgwood to her class for design presentations; this favour was often returned.

Mairi's parents were John MacBride and Anne MacKinnon. Anne MacKinnon was born on August 30th 1869 at Lee, Bunessan, Isle of Mull, and died on Boxing Day 1946 at the age of seventy-seven. John MacBride was born on April 27th 1872 at 209 Duke Street, Glasgow. In the 1891 Govanhill census, at the age of eighteen, he is listed as a sewing machine mechanic. He is also described variously as an engine fitter, journeyman, exciseman, spirit storeman, engine fitter and bond warehouse manager. It was known that he went to sea and spent some time in America; on his return he opened an inn on the shores of Loch Ness, where his wife Anne also worked as cook.

Mairi had three siblings: Angus MacBride (my grandfather, affectionately known as 'Papa'), Anna MacBride ('Dolly') and Stewart MacBride. Angus was born on September 27th 1898 and died on June 8th 1969. He married Sarah More and they had three children: the eldest was my mother, Sheila MacBride.

Mairi with brother-in-law Edmund and sister Anna, niece Sheila and great-niece Anne in 1957

Annie Thomson MacBride was born January 26th 1902 at Camphill, Paisley. She died on June 11th 1997. She was known as 'Aunty Dolly' and later became known as Anna Hart.

Stewart MacBride was born October 26th 1904 at Camphill, Paisley but tragically died in infancy. The story was that he died of fright when the foghorn sounded while he was aboard the steamship *Dunara Castle*. According to the records for Deaths at Sea—Marine Register, the death occurred on June 30th 1905 when the ship was off Colonsay (number 70319). It was reported that Stewart, aged just eight months, had died of tubercular disease. Thus, he must have had an inherent weakness from this illness.

Mairi's house Duntulm,
Salen, in around 1960

Mairi lived most of her life at a house called Duntulm, in Salen. My mother and father met during the war years in Salen, while my mother was staying at Duntulm with her siblings, Angus and Fiona. They had come to stay with their aunt and grandmother on Mull, to escape the bombing in Glasgow. My father, Robert MacDonald, was born and brought up in Salen. He was the son of the local doctors, Flora and Reginald.

Duntulm is one of a row of houses on the right as you enter Salen from the east. Our family lived next door in a house called Rockville. Mairi, my great aunt, was always known affectionately as 'Aunty Bunty'.

Fiona Somerled

Preface

A quarter century—twenty-five years, two and a half decades—is a long time, no matter how you look at it or count it up. When you consider that it is over a third of one's 'threescore years and ten' it is indeed a very long time, for me, that I have lived with cancer.

A doctor friend suggested that I should write about my life as a cancer sufferer, but knowing people's dread of the word—never mind the disease itself—I asked him who would read such a book, and his reply was 'You would be surprised.' He even suggested a title: *My Quarter Century Living With Cancer*.

The cancer consultant, when I told him of my plans, thought the idea an excellent one and told me to get on with it. Both of these medical men agreed that my story would help take the fear out of the word 'cancer' for all hale and hearty people, and give hope and courage to cancer sufferers.

Never having written a book before, I am at a complete loss how to begin. Everything has a beginning, a middle and an end. For me though, where does the beginning start—with birth? Conception, maybe? As I am still alive at time of writing I know nothing about the end, so I suppose I should start in the middle—the middle that was the half century of my life.

Contents

1

Cancer Number One

Mairi aged about 50

I think it would be within a week or so of my fiftieth birthday, my half century, when I accidentally found I had a very small lump on my left breast. I was leaning forward over the back of a chair when I realised that the chair back was pressing on a sensitive area. There was no pain, I was just conscious of a something—I did not know what.

When having my bath that night, I felt around the area and discovered the lump fairly deep within the breast but not visible. As I had been attending the doctor about a bloodless condition and was due to get a new supply of pills, I mentioned my small lump to him. Now I was approaching the menopause, when glands sometimes act strangely, so the doctor said it might be a gland but that he would keep an eye on it.

Cancer at this time did not enter my head and it was not until my second visit, when the doctor said he thought I should see a specialist, that I started to have misgivings.

At this point I should tell you something about myself, my job, social life and background. I was teaching at an art college in a Midlands city. Over the years I had worked up to my present post—that of Head of the Dress Design Department—by teaching drawing, painting and design, historic ornament, the history of costume, and most of the crafts. During the war, with so many males in the Forces, I had to turn my hand to anything and everything for which I was qualified.

My social life was just beginning to pick up where the war years had broken it off. One of the societies to which I belonged was the Scottish Caledonian Society, and as there is no Scot so 'clannish' as the exiled Scot, we met—and let our hair down—at the Burns dinner and St Andrew's night. You might wonder what all this has to do with cancer, the two things being poles apart ... but two members of that society were to play an important role in my life. An eminent surgeon was the first (I will refer to him as 'Mr X') and the second was a radiologist. When my GP told me I should see a specialist about my lump, I naturally asked to be sent to Mr X. I was told that if I wanted to see a consultant of my own choice, I would need to visit him at his surgery as a private patient and not at the hospital—and this was arranged, for I definitely wanted to see Mr X.

Mairi's niece Sheila in Paris, 1950

I saw the surgeon within a week and he confirmed that I did indeed have a lump on my breast, and that it would require surgery to have it investigated. It so happened that my college Whitsun break was almost due and I had booked to go to Paris with a friend, and was taking my niece Sheila with me. I knew that if I entered the hospital just then the holiday would have to be cancelled, which apart from being a disappointment to me, would be a very big disappointment to the two young people. I explained this to the consultant and asked his advice. He remained silent for a bit, then he looked into my eyes and said, 'Yes, have your Paris holiday and enter hospital immediately on your return'—ten days in all. So, to Paris we went.

It was a first visit for all three of us, dreamed about and saved for over the years, and what a time we had! It is seldom that reality exceeds the dream but on this occasion, it did. We went in and out of shops and art galleries, spent an evening at the Folies Bergère, walked the full length of the Champs-Élysées from the Arc de Triomphe to the Place de la Concorde, and went to the top of the Eiffel Tower and Sacré-Coeur.

At the end of the holiday I reported to the surgeon, who had booked a bed for me in the private ward at the hospital. I occupied the bed within days and the surgeon told me to think of and relive my Paris trip rather than focusing on what the operation might prove. He told me exactly what he intended doing: that was, to remove a piece of tissue with the lump, send it to the pathologist and if all went well, that would be the end of it. I told him not to do that but to remove the whole breast, if he was in any doubt or thought that it would be safer to do so. I also made him promise to tell me, good or bad, the results of the pathologist's report—and this he agreed to do. Later he told me that it was the smallest lump he had ever removed, no bigger than a pea, but that it was pre-malignant. He also told me that I was the only patient he ever had who, facing a possible cancer, had asked to go to Paris prior to the operation!

As the lump was pre-malignant, it was thought advisable that I should have what was then called 'deep ray treatment'. The specialist in this department was the other member of the Caledonian Society I mentioned. I saw this doctor and we discussed both the treatment and what was to be expected from it. If I remember rightly I was to have fifteen exposures, and as my operation had been on the 10th June and the college summer holidays began in the middle of July, I was anxious to get the treatment over and return home to my beloved Hebrides as soon as possible. The doctor, being a fellow Scot, understood how I felt and said that he would do his best but it would mean having the deep ray treatment before my wound was healed.

As soon as I was well enough, the treatment began. Parts of my chest, back and side were marked with a blue pencil, pinpointing where the rays from the machine were to beam. The room where I had the treatment was small, with a tiny window on the opposite wall from the door. In the centre of the room and clearly visible from the window was a table, and above that, a huge monster-like machine with a long moveable arm. I was positioned lying on the table. Packed around the marked area were small bags which left exposed the parts where the rays were to beam. I never thought to ask what the bags contained but from the feel of them, their size and weight, they reminded me of two-pound bags of sugar. The machine was lowered until it was just inches above my body; the movable arm was directed over the exposed areas then the door was shut tightly as the radiologist left me, and I was alone. I had been told not to move, but to remain as steady as possible. I was so afraid that I might cough or sneeze, and concentrated so hard on not doing either, that the eight minutes passed and I recollected afterwards that I had forgotten to be afraid! Anyhow, I knew that I was being observed all the time through the window, so what was there to be afraid of? There was a gentle hum when the machine was switched on, and it was several minutes after it was switched off and the hum ceased before the door was opened and the radiologist returned. This, I learned later, was a radiation safeguard for the machine operator. I had this treatment every second day and throughout that time the only ill effect was a tendency to experience nausea about one or two hours after each treatment.

After the last session, the doctor asked me how soon I could get home to the Island of Mull if I travelled the next day. On being told that it would take two days with a break of journey for one night in Glasgow, he stressed that I had to be home and in the care of my own doctor by the fourth day following the treatment, as I would have a very sore arm—very sore indeed, and similar to a severe burn. He gave me some ointment to apply to the arm, back and chest, and instructed me to report back to him at the end of my holiday. He said that the good Mull air, plus the personal care of the family doctor, would do me more good than any tonic—and how right he was!

On the morning of the fourth day, safe in my own bed, with a breathtaking view of the hills from my bedroom window, I awakened to find that I had a very painful and badly swollen arm and side. Now, in the Hebrides, the doctor is not just someone who keeps surgery hours and dispenses pills and bottles of medicine when required. He is also everybody's friend, be you well or ill. He has the time to talk to everyone and so every door is open to him at all times.

Our doctor[1] was a keen fisherman and when he got a good catch everyone in the village shared it. What care he took of me during those two weeks. I suffered so much pain from the deep ray burns! For his compassion and gentleness—when changing the dressings, and when I unashamedly wept—I shall always remember him with love and gratitude. The dressings were four-inch Vaseline petroleum gauze squares which always stuck to the open wound and the broken burns on my skin. The removal of these dressings in order to apply fresh ones daily was indeed painful. But, like everything else, pain does not last forever.

As was the custom in our part of the world, when there was illness, that illness was everyone's concern, with the result that friends and neighbours—and indeed it seemed at the time the whole world—brought me nourishing gifts of chickens, rabbits, freshly churned butter, fish straight from the sea and, judging by the colour, some from the mouth of a river (but by mutual understanding one never enquired about the latter; if a little poaching was done in order to tempt my appetite, who was to say it was wrong?)

An English friend, with whose family I stayed, travelled north with me and as she also was a teacher and had long summer holidays, she stayed on to look after me. Poor girl, she little knew what she was letting herself in for! Her knowledge of a fowl or a rabbit was of something one saw in a poulterer's window or when served on a plate at table, never a dead thing in its feathers or fur. The first one handed in she eyed with dismay, brought it to me in my bedroom and enquired what she should do with it. I asked her to help me into my dressing gown, and I would sit in the kitchenette and instruct her step by step, and this we did. Recalling the scene in the kitchenette during the next couple of hours made me rock with mirth ... I do not know if you have ever plucked or dressed a fowl in your life; if you have not, then the way to do it is to pluck against the lie of the feathers—that is, from tail to neck. By the time Alys had plucked that bird, there were feathers in her hair and in every corner of the kitchenette. Added to this she discovered that fowls have lice, so every few minutes she opened the back door for a breath of air. While the air revived her, it also scattered the feathers. When the plucking stage was over, I showed her how to hold the fowl over a flame to singe it, killing any lice and destroying the odd feather. By the time her holiday was over—if it can be called one—that lass could rival any farm wife in dressing fowls, skinning rabbits or gutting fish!

An amusing incident happened one day when an old man came to the door to enquire how I was. Now the old man was very Highland and the girl very English and although they both spoke in English, neither understood a word the other said. They talked at cross purposes for some time and much to my amusement, for the conversation was most enlightening: the one talking about my health while the other—mistaking the term 'herself' to mean the Queen—wondered if the Queen was ill! Eventually, speaking in Gaelic, I called downstairs to the neighbour to come up and see me. My friend told me afterwards that old Neil had shoved a pair of rabbits into her hands, bounded up the stairs two at a time (he would have been nearer eighty than seventy) and had looked at her as though she were an idiot! Alys learned a lot that summer of how country folk live, how to bake a girdle scone and pancakes ... for although I could not do these jobs myself, I could and did teach her how to do them. I owe that girl a debt of gratitude.

With all the nourishment and everyone's loving care, I soon got my strength back.

1. Dr Reginald MacDonald, who is mentioned in the Foreword. Dr MacDonald died in 1953.

2

The Cushion, the Inflatable & the Malpas

On my return to college in September 1950 my principal said that he wanted me to put on a mannequin parade in November, as part of the entertainment at the prize-giving. As head of the department, I had all the arrangements to make: to select materials, pass sketches, get my assistants to make up toiles from the sketches, and my senior students to make up and model the garments. There were endless rehearsals, timing the girls on the catwalk, making sure they walked tall and turned gracefully. I shall never know how I managed to put on that show, for I still had an open wound in my chest. The evening came at last, the show went on, and I stood in the wings. I looked each girl over before she went on and gave each one a word of encouragement. When it was over, my girls crowded around me; seeing how wonderful they felt, with their happy faces,

I forgot just how tired I was until my principal sent me home in a taxi.

Life then went on much as usual. I had no time to feel sorry for myself, for no matter how tired I often felt, I had to earn my living and had the upkeep of my home on Mull—and lodgings in England too—to pay for. One of my greatest problems at this time, and one that afforded me a lot of amusement, was the matter of an artificial breast. My bust measurement had been thirty-five inches, so my breasts needed good support. My first artificial breast, matching my own in size as closely as possible, was made of some sort of material usually used to stuff cushions. I cannot remember how much I paid for it, or indeed for any of the others, for the 'cushion' was to be the first of many. I made a pocket on the inside of my bra to insert it into. The thing looked all right first thing in the morning when I left home for the college but by mid-morning, being lighter in weight than my own breast, the cushion had worked up and out of the pocket and was about a couple of inches or so below my chin—while without proper balance, my own breast sank until it was only a few inches above my waist, or so I thought. So to hold down the artificial breast I made little bags, inserted lead weights, placed the bags in the bra pocket along with the cushion and hoped for the best.

Mairi wearing one of her own creations, July 1957

As a teacher of dress design, part of my job was to give my students a passing acquaintance with anatomy in order that they would design a garment that was functional, one that the wearer could get on and off. I taught them that the human body was rounded, and that bones played an important part when the design for a garment was being created. Also, when making a sketch of their design, the figure would look ungainly if the model stood with the balance equally divided with the weight on both feet. So models were made to stand with the weight on one foot. This had the effect of the line of the shoulders and bust going in one direction, and the line of the hips and knees going in the opposite direction, with the 'gap' taking place at the waist. I suggest you try this yourself by standing in front of a long mirror.

Use a ruler, held horizontally, with your eyes half closed. Now, open your eyes and observe the slight angle the ruler has taken when held in line with the shoulders. Do the same across the bust and the ruler will follow the same line. Now move down to the hips and you will find that the ruler angle is in the opposite direction. Had it not been for the above knowledge, I would have been less aware of my lopsided breast. When my shoulders and own breast went in one direction, my cushion breast remained, without movement, steady and solid like the Rock of Gibraltar!

Ask any woman who has lost one breast what her reactions were when she looked at herself in a mirror, and I feel sure that the answer will be loss of confidence in herself because she is so aware of her one-sidedness.

The 'cushion' was breast number one ... breast number two, I bought in a surgical appliance shop in Glasgow, and it was made of inflatable rubber. I had to blow it up until it was the same size as my own breast but as the tube was at the side the task was somewhat difficult, for when blown up the tube had to be secured with a cap to keep the air in, like a balloon. Really, a gymnastic feat if ever there was one! In my job I naturally worked a lot with pins, as a toile was draped on a model during the designing stage of a garment being fitted. Some people put pins in their mouth between the lips, as a shoemaker does with nails—but I always stuck the pins in front of my bosom. Yes, you have guessed what happened. I stuck a pin into the inflatable rubber breast ... and with a hissing noise, the wretched thing collapsed! I retired to the ladies as quickly as possible, unrolled the toilet paper, bunched it up, put it in a handkerchief and stuffed it in the bra pocket!

Breast number three was called a Malpas: a circular bag half-filled with granules which looked like grains of sugar. The idea was that being only partly filled, the bag remained in place but the granules moved. So if I was in a reclining or horizontal position the breast became more or less flat. When I was upright, the granules fell as a normal breast would. I congratulated myself on at last having found the ideal artificial breast—but my troubles were far from over. Bust sizes, for some unknown reason, go up or down by two inches, never by one inch. As my bust was thirty-five inches, I had to buy a thirty-six-inch size, open it up and spoon out some of the granules until I arrived at what I thought was about right.

I was a member of the Soroptimist Club, a kind of female Rotary Club with only one member eligible from each profession, and that member had to be the top one in her sphere. Being a Soroptimist meant that I was involved in a host of social activities, at many of which—such as dinners of our own club and neighbouring clubs—I had to wear full evening dress. Fortunately, I was able to design and make my own dresses, so I designed them to suit my disfigurements—the artificial breast and the blotches on my upper arm and chest left by the deep ray treatment. I got over the blotches quite easily by cutting the dress fairly high under the arms and hoping I would not need to raise my arm higher than shoulder level. To camouflage the breast was a bit more difficult but I overcame this by cutting the bodice asymmetrically, by draping, or by attaching a hand-made spray of flowers, making sure that the leaves were arranged so that one covered the lump of loose flesh that had been stitched up and resembled a miniature mountain (or so it appeared to me). Another leaf was pulled towards the centre of my chest to hide where I fell away showing the gap between me, the artificial breast and the dress.

Latterly I was the first Vice President of our club, and this meant that a press photograph was taken of the club officials, guests from other clubs, and City guests—including the Lord Mayor and Lady Mayoress, town clerk, and so on. Now if there is anything peculiar about your person you can be sure it will show up in a photograph!

Looking over those old photographs now, no one would ever know that I was lopsided.

Sometime after my first operation, I met my surgeon at a Burns dinner. After the usual greetings were exchanged he remarked that he had not seen me for a while. When I replied that the less I saw of him the better he looked at me for a second, then it dawned on him what I meant! He told me that he always enquired about me when he met the radiologist and that he was told I was 'doing well'.

During the years that followed I attended the radiotherapy department regularly. The two-month intervals to begin with were gradually increased to three, six, and nine months and, eventually, a year. At this time I was naturally worried lest the cancer should spread. It was in fact a primary with no secondaries, but I did not know this at the time.

We who are Highland have some strange beliefs such as premonitions, second sight and interpreting dreams. One night I had a dream (or perhaps I should say it was in the early hours of the morning just before awakening, for that is the dream with meaning)—I dreamt I had a conversation with my mother. My mother had died in 1946 and was buried in Pennygown graveyard on the Island of Mull, one of the most beautiful sites for a burial ground in the whole world. Within its hallowed grounds there is a twelfth-century roofless chapel, the whole enclosed in a drystone wall. In my dream I was sitting on the wall with my mother, looking towards the sea, that wonderful stretch of water known as the Sound of Mull (*Caol Muile*). We conversed in Gaelic and my mother told me not to worry about my 'lump', as it would never take me to the graveyard.

In the morning I had little time to think about my dream. After all, who in a city gives much or any thought to dreams? Yet as the day wore on, the memory of my dream kept recurring in my mind. Now the strange thing is that being in England for so long and speaking only English, my Gaelic was a bit rusty—so if anyone had asked me the day before what the Gaelic word for 'graveyard' was I would have replied that I did not know, graveyard being a word not often used in everyday conversation. I was so surprised that my subconscious mind had remembered, when my conscious mind had forgotten, that I looked it up in the Gaelic dictionary and found that the word was correct. Correct also was my mother's prediction that my breast cancer would not be the cause of my death. I felt safe and reassured about that.

That was Cancer Number One.

3

Radio Broadcast

During the summer of 1953, I was asked to do a broadcast for a radio programme. It was funny really, how I came to do the broadcast—as I did not want to do it at first, being very busy spring cleaning the house and not feeling that I had any time to write a script. One morning there was a knock at the front door. I was doing a washing in the kitchenette and so asked one of my nieces to answer the door and find out who was there. My niece came back and said that a man and a woman wanted to see me. She had invited them in, and they were awaiting me in the lounge.

The man said he was from the BBC and introduced the woman as his secretary. He said that as I was the only native artist belonging to the island and as they were going to record interviews with various people to be broadcast during the winter, would I tell him something of the beauty of Mull and describe a particular view which I kept in my mind's eye when exiled in England. Well, as I said already, I was in the middle of a washing, the day was good and I was anxious to get the clothes out on the line as soon as possible. However, he assured me I would not need to write a script; the secretary would write down everything I said and that would be that.

Mairi's favourite view, 'Gualann Dhubh', on the road from Salen to Tobermory, Isle of Mull—Photo courtesy of Mairi's niece, Anne Barr

Now if there is one thing I like better than anything else it is to describe the beauty that is Mull! So I described a view that took in the whole Sound of Mull—the panoramic view from Gualann Dhubh, the highest point on the road from Salen to Tobermory, with Ardnamurchan in the west and Ben Cruachan in the east. Dotted between, there were the Green Islands, the Grey Islands and Lismore. On the Morvern side, there was also a wonderful stretch from Drimnin to Lochaline and beyond.

My second view, which I loved to remember, was from midway across the Sound of Iona between Fionnphort and Iona, where looking north were the hills of Skye and Rhum, and looking south, the Torrin Rocks, the Paps of Jura and on a good day, a glimpse of Islay. I asked the man, whose name I have forgotten, which view he wanted and he answered 'both'. He told me his secretary had noted all that I had said and that they would return the following morning, read the script over to me to ensure it was exactly what

I had said and if correct, they would record it. Then I got back to my washing.

The following day as I was doing the ironing about half a dozen men arrived, including the man who had interviewed me, and his secretary. I was handed a script, asked to read it—which I did—and found it to be correct, word for word.

It was decided that the microphone would stand on a small table in the lounge with a cable connecting it to the recording van outside, by way of the window. I was told that I would possibly have to rehearse it several times depending on how my voice recorded, so the best thing to do was for me to read one sentence from the script, stop, then wait until they spoke to me. Meantime the engineers in the recording van would replay the one sentence, listen to how it sounded and would then tell me whether to go straight ahead or whether it would require to be re-rehearsed. Now the three girls, my two nieces and a friend who was staying with me, were standing in the hall listening, but they did not know about the arrangement for me to read only one sentence and stop. So when I finished the first sentence and then there was silence they said to each other, 'Oh, she has fainted!' and were just about to burst into the room when they heard me start again from the beginning and read the script right through.

Out in the van afterwards the engineers played the recording back to me but I have no recollection of what I said or how I said it, I was so shocked by the strange sound of my own voice!

The girls gave everyone coffee and all thoughts of finishing the ironing had gone out of my head, as I was still stunned from meeting a complete stranger and hearing my own voice, which I had lived with for fifty years yet did not know!

The sequel to the tale happened almost a year later. I normally went abroad for the Whitsun holiday, but this time I decided to go to Mull. I booked a sleeper on the Euston to Oban night train and joined the service at Crewe. The conductor told me that I could choose any bunk, and that two ladies would be joining me at Preston. I decided on the top bunk and that as I was tired I would not speak to my fellow travellers when they entered the compartment—and this I did. The following morning the conductor brought us tea and, to be sociable, I asked my companions where they were travelling to. On being told they were going to Oban I said that I was going there also, whereupon they said that they were really going to Mull, so I told them that I too was going to Mull. They had never been there before and whether out of curiosity or just to make conversation I do not know, but I asked them why they had chosen Mull rather than, say, Skye, which was a more widely known island. Their reply left me speechless for a minute when they said that in Manchester they had listened to a programme on the radio about Mull, and a woman had described how very beautiful it was. When I said I was that woman, I do not know which of us was the most surprised!

Naturally, I now felt responsible for them so spent the rest of the journey pointing out places of particular beauty or of historical interest, such as the Pass of Brander where the battle was fought when then MacDougall of MacDougall got so near to Robert the Bruce that he was able to grasp the plaid brooch worn by Bruce and tear it from the weave. The brooch is now in the possession of the MacDougall chief of the clan, and it is my proud boast that I held it once in my hands. Then there was Oban to show them, for we had nearly four hours between train and boat.

On the boat (which for a change neither rocked, pitched nor rolled) there was much to point out: the view up Loch Linnhe to Ben Nevis, past Lismore with its lighthouse and water turbulence; the Lady's Rock and the story behind its name; Duart Castle, and the beautiful romantic mountains of Mull itself. How pleased I was to be going home! Like the song, 'Westering Home', the sheer beauty of it would bring tears to your eyes; such is my island, and the 'my' is indeed possessive.

4

Teaching

During the next few years I got on with the job of living, and led a normal life. I taught four full days a week, plus three evenings. All the staff had to do evening classes, for which we were given one free day each week. Part of my job was to take a small group of senior students to London every March before their examinations, in order to visit art galleries, shops and dress shows. The college booked a reasonably-priced hotel for us and all other plans and arrangements were left with me.

As this was the highlight of the four-year course to the National Diploma it received a great deal of thought and attention. Every student planned well in advance what they would wear. All decided on new shoes. While I encouraged them to choose the theatre we would go to, or the ballet, or shops, or galleries, I never mentioned shoes—and the reason why will be apparent presently.

I always wrote to one of the top dress designers for permission to view their collection, and chose a different designer each year, giving an assurance that no sketching of models would be done. Permission was always granted, graciously, and on arrival at the salon we would be conducted to an upstairs room, greeted by ladies who were more accustomed to duchesses—certainly to no one below the wife or daughter of a sheik or millionaire. Sometimes we were even greeted by the great man himself!

The salon was always beautiful, with flowers, glistening chandeliers, expensive curtains, thick carpets and gilt chairs to sit on. We barely had two pennies to rub together, but we felt like millionaires. Top models were used to show off the collection and although the designer and all his staff knew we were not buyers, they all treated us as though we were. Some of the dresses shown to us cost at that time £500.

Our stay in London lasted for three nights. By day, we went to the galleries and shops, and at night we went to the theatre or just walked around the city. When walking around, I always wore comfortable old shoes. My girls, however, wore their new ones—with the result that by bedtime their feet were so sore and swollen that when they said 'Goodnight', I knew they were in bed unable to take another step. Thus, I could go to my own room without worrying if the girls were safe indoors in the hotel. Cruel? Perhaps!

Each girl during the visit would concentrate on different parts of a garment: one on necklines and collars, one on bodices, one on skirts. Then between five o'clock and dinner at half past seven, they were left on their own to pool their ideas and each create a garment. Over dinner, I studied their sketches and we discussed fashion trends and almost everything from cabbages to kings. You are perhaps wondering what I was doing between 5 p.m. and 7.30? I expect you have guessed—I was in bed with my feet on a pillow, getting ready for our nightly walk ... when we were not going to the theatre. Down Regent Street, along Piccadilly (with a long look at the neon lights and Eros), up Bond Street and along Oxford Street, and so on—I saw London by night. I also made quite sure that I had every girl at my side, or within sight.

One of the highlights of the visit was buying a hat for myself. I always bought the hat at Harrods and always paid more than I could afford for it, but I considered the cost small when compared to the pleasure it gave the girls. There I would sit, on a stool, with mirrors everywhere that I might see myself from every angle. The girls were also given stools to sit on, and freely gave their opinions on all the model hats the assistant brought for me to try on. The girls were not allowed to handle the hats, but would point to one on a stand and exclaim, 'Oh Miss! Try this one!' until I had tried on nearly every hat in the shop. Fortunately the assistants entered into the spirit of the adventure and never once made us feel that we were 'country cousins come to town'. I usually spent more on that hat than I did on the whole of my wardrobe for the rest of the year! When we returned home, every time I wore it the girls invariably said, 'You are wearing our hat!' I do not think they ever noticed my face ... just the hat!

On one occasion I was invited to a dress show at Bradford College of Art, which I accepted, and I took three senior students with me. At this time I had a male student named Brian. He had designed a dress for his mother and was in the process of making it, so he was the only student I was afraid to leave to work on his own—particularly as the dress had a bound buttonhole on the bodice part. The rest of the class assured me that they would look after him, and not to worry.

I heard afterwards that about the middle of the morning one of the girls asked Brian how he was getting on with his pocket. He told them it was not a pocket but a buttonhole, and proudly displayed it. The girls were aghast when they saw the buttonhole, fully five inches long, and the button only one and a half inches in diameter! They held a hurried conference and decided that as the material was reversible and the dress asymmetrical, they could cut a new half front bodice from the scraps. Between them, they remade the whole bodice with a perfect buttonhole!

Of course I knew nothing of this until weeks later. Not a word was said when I returned—not even when I scolded them for having done so little work and complemented Brian on his beautiful buttonhole. When I was eventually told the story I was asked to promise not to scold Brian because it was their fault really, for not looking after him as they had assured me they would. I asked the girls what Brian was doing while they were doing his work and was told he had calmly taken out his pipe, lit it and sat in a corner out of the way, quietly smoking.

Brian was a German Jew whose family had fled from Germany when Hitler was in power, prior to the war. After the war he returned to Germany and when he revisited England he came to see me. Among other things, he told me that he was now a successful dress designer in Germany, in charge of a workroom of about fifty men and women. I wonder how he coped when one of them made a mistake—would he remember how everyone had helped him and shown him tolerance? A strange thing about my job was that when old students came back to see me (and most of them did) the ones who went on to teach only earned about one third of the salary of the ones who went into industry. Funny old world!

Burslem College of Art—Photo courtesy of Steven Birks

Teaching is what you make it—a joy or a chore. I loved it, and I loved all my students; they gave me their best and I knew that I had their respect and affection. Many were the explosive and amusing incidents we shared ... like the day of the accident with the basin of water. It should never have happened, but happen it did—and it was all my own fault. A student, busy creating a design, had called to me to come and have a look at it. So, I had the sketch in one hand, with some adjusting to do to the toile on the stand. I knew that there was a chair directly behind me, because it was always there, and I decided that as I was about to enter into a lengthy discussion I might as well sit down. I took a few steps backwards and sat, plonk, in the middle of a basin of water! A girl had been using a damp cloth for pressing and for convenience had placed the basin on the chair!

There was an intake of breath, then sudden silence. I was speechless and so were they. I looked at their horrified faces and, realising the whole farcical situation, I burst out laughing and demanded to know why they were standing about instead of lending a hand to get me out of my unwanted bath. There was a rush to help, the girls laughing hesitantly at first, then real mirth took over and our laughter was completely out of control! They tugged and pulled at both me and the basin and I finally became separated from it, but not before I was soaked to the skin. The girls were magnificent ... I was undressed by many hands and as each garment was stripped off me, one of them ran to a radiator with it to try and dry it. Every garment below the waist had to be removed; the upper ones remained quite dry, fortunately! One girl thoughtfully removed her own waist slip, so covering my lower regions while the drying process was going on. Another kept watch at the door and another stationed herself on the stairs to give a warning signal to the girl at the door, should any male member of staff appear. What should have been a serious lesson ended up a hilarious pantomime. Years later, I met one of the girls from that class—a teacher by this time—and she told me that when they saw that I was going to sit down on the usual chair, they were all so petrified that none of them could utter a word of warning!

The other side of teaching, apart from the actual job, was giving my students some confidence just before they entered the examination room. They were all given a pep talk in advance, told to start the paper with the question they could answer best and to work in that order always, leaving the question they were most unsure about to the last and to make an intelligent start to it by writing—or sketching—a small part of the answer. This would give them an extra half mark at least, and every half mark counted. Further, the examiner would not know whether they knew the answer, or had run out of time!

Before the examination, some girls wept with nerves and I had to take them to my own room to calm them, wipe their faces with a damp towel to hide the traces of tears, and tell them that all that was expected of them was their best and that no one could better their best. If they failed, what did it matter; people learned from their failures, and not from their successes. I had confidence in them, and they must have confidence in themselves. Some said that the presence of the invigilator put every creative idea out of their head. Then I would tell them to pretend that I was sitting in the invigilator's seat willing them to do their best. Some of my students told me afterwards that they had done this and it worked!

Later, when examinations were over and I had access to the question papers, we had a post-mortem session of question and answer. When asked how they had got on, the reply was always the same—'Awful!'—but the post-mortem showed that my confidence in them was justified.

I have always believed that God in His wisdom never gives us a burden too heavy to carry, but He will give us one until we are fully stretched. Therefore, it was with this belief firmly in my mind that I faced my second cancer.

5

Cancer Number Two

Out of the blue in February 1958 I had a showing of blood. Being long past the menopause, I realised that there was something far wrong and went along to see the doctor the following morning. He thought there might be nothing to worry about; it could be something quite simple like a polyp. After all, my breast cancer was a primary with no secondaries. However, he thought I ought to see a gynaecologist. I was told that the hospital would contact me and I would be given an appointment. I asked the doctor how long I would have to wait for the appointment and I was told quite a time as there was a long waiting list, unless of course I wanted to go privately. I said I would wait, but I had no sooner left the consulting room than I had second thoughts. I told the receptionist when I returned to the waiting room that I wanted to go back to see the doctor. Because of cancer number one being very much in my mind the doctor understood how I felt about speed in the matter, and so there and then he made an appointment by phone for me to see the gynaecologist within a week. As medical ethics will not permit me to mention the name of the gynaecologist, I will refer to him as 'Mr B'.

Mr B said that as I only had one showing of blood it could well be a polyp, but it would need surgery to remove it. I told him that I wanted it done as soon as possible and it was arranged that I should go into hospital the following week as a private patient, have the minor operation, and be home within seven days.

After the operation, I would have been back at home only for about a week when a doctor friend called to see me and told me that I had to go back to the hospital the following day, for major surgery. How my friend came to be my informant was a bit unusual. While I had been in hospital she had visited me. When the pathologist's report came through and the hospital had to get in touch with me immediately, the ward sister remembered my doctor friend and, as I was not on the phone myself, she had phoned my friend and had asked her to give me the message that I was to report to the hospital the next morning for an urgent operation. I knew the meaning of the message and my heart sank, for here was my second cancer—and a hysterectomy loomed.

Following the hysterectomy, having had two operations within ten days, I was very ill for a time. My sister came down from Scotland to be near me and one night, just after the operation, she was told to wait on after visiting hours as my pulse was very low. She told me later that the doctors and nurses kept a close watch on me and checked my pulse at frequent intervals. Then at about 4 a.m. the registrar came in, took my pulse again, and told my sister that she could go home as my pulse was stronger and I would pull through.

I took a long time to get over the hysterectomy, was very weak and had no appetite. The water I had been given to sip was tepid and I had a great longing for a really cold drink. Now, on my grandfather's ground on Mull there was a spring of crystal clear water, cold and pure from the mountain from which it sprang. A drink from that spring was health-giving, and for days I could think of nothing but that spring of water! The more I thought about it, the more determined I became to get on my feet and take the long road home to Mull.

While in bed at the hospital after the operations I had a showing of blood, which concerned me. I mentioned it to the sister, who just said not to worry—but worry I did. So when the consultant was doing his rounds one day, I decided to tell him myself when he came to my bedside. He listened, studied my face all the time, then patted my hand and said it was all right. His touch was reassuring and I felt relaxed as I watched him continue on his rounds.

As you know, when a consultant goes on his rounds he is accompanied by his assistant houseman, sister, nurses and anyone else studying medicine who happens to be around. However on this day, when Mr B finished his round he looked back to my bed. Whether he was conscious that my eyes were following him I'll never know, but on reaching the ward door he dismissed those around him, came back and sat on my bed. He told me exactly why I had the showing of blood and explained in detail how, during an operation, the severed blood vessels had to be tied and if the knot was not tight enough, sometimes blood would seep through until healing took place. He also told me that my new cancer, although malignant, was another primary, and as everything had been removed there was no need to worry; and he added that while I was on the operating table they had had a good look around and were quite satisfied of that. He said that it was not everyone who could be told they had one cancer, and I was hearing it for the second time; he was telling me because he felt I had an inner strength and could take it. There we were, a Christian and a Jew, in tune with each other and having a heart to heart talk. Years later I heard that he had died of a disease rare in a man. Jew or Gentile, there would be a place awaiting him in heaven, of that I am certain.

When I was out of danger, I was moved from the little side room into the main ward. I was feeling low that first day and could not be bothered to be sociable, so I kept my eyes shut and feigned sleep. The other women in the ward must have been wondering what was the nature of my trouble, for the two of them came to the foot of my bed to study my chart which was hanging there. Imagine my surprise when one said to the other, 'I do not know what is wrong with her, but she has had a Presbyterian'. As everyone else had either 'Methodist', 'Roman Catholic' or 'Church of England' on their charts, they had possibly never heard the word 'Presbyterian' before, and had concluded that my religion was my illness!

Although not too uncomfortable after the hysterectomy, my general health was low. I found that I was weepy, which is a well-known condition following that surgery. When the visiting hour was over I used to put my head under the bedclothes so that no one would see me, and have a good cry. Then one day I discovered that every woman in the ward did the same thing! 'Hysterectomy', 'hysterics'—both words come from the Greek word *hystera*, meaning 'the womb' (with which hysteria was formerly thought to be connected), and so it was not surprising that we were all weepy. If anyone had said an unkind word to me or given me an unkind look, it would have broken my heart! When I started to walk around again I found that I was afraid to stand up straight and always supported myself by placing a hand on either side of my abdomen, as though I expected my stomach to fall out!

Well, that was my second cancer. I had lost my womb, but in this there was nothing to regret. It had never fulfilled its function, never held a foetus and had never produced a child.

I never did have the time to ponder the question of whether I felt deprived or cheated out of what could have been a wonderful experience. My hands were always full, looking after and caring for other people's children and young people. My brother's children, Sheila, Angus and Fiona, had come to Mull at the outbreak of World War II to escape the bombing in Glasgow, and so I had a hand in their upbringing. I was not only their Aunty, but also Aunty to all their friends and indeed, to half the children in the village at that time! I never thought I spoiled any one of them but I must have done in some measure for years later, Robin (Sheila's husband and the son of our own two local doctors) placed his baby daughter in my arms and said, 'Here is your great-niece, and do not spoil her as you spoiled your nieces!'

6

Retirement

At some time in every life we are touched by the hand of death—whether in our own family circle or with the severing of a well-loved friendship.

As a very small child I had thought of death with horror—of being placed in a box, stuck in the ground and then both me and the box being covered over with earth. I just knew that I would suffocate. Later, when I was a bit older, I realised that I could not suffocate for dead people can no longer breathe—so that was a relief. Still, there were always the worms! I knew it was wicked to feel afraid, for when someone died they went to a wonderful place called heaven, so what was there to be afraid of? Well for a start, no one had ever explained how I should get out of the box to get to heaven. At this point I would shut my mind, put the thought of death as far from me as possible, and tell myself that I would have it all made clear to me when I grew up.

While lying in hospital I wondered about the parts of me that had ended up in the furnace. I had felt no pain, therefore God's spirit did not live in any one part of me—and yet lived within me. What a comforting thought. I had been given a spirit with which to face the ups and downs of life, and while that spirit was a part of me, I would live. So I would get on with the job of living.

I was physically weak and would dearly have loved to stop working and enjoy the years that were left to me. Owing to a superannuation problem I could not retire before the end of January 1961, when I would qualify for a small teacher's pension. I would have my own house to retire to, the old family home, fully furnished and well-equipped and sitting in a half acre of ground. So, I would be housed and that was no problem. I would, however, have rates, heating, lighting and the upkeep of the house—the latter a must on a gale-swept island. Then of course, I would have to eat.

Sometimes, when I was particularly tired after a long day—having left the flat at 8.30 a.m. and not returning home until 9.30 p.m.—I would crawl into bed, get up after an hour's rest, make a meal, prepare for the following morning and have a good wash, often too tired to sleep. At such times I would go over my capital and assets and try and work out how long they would last me, without an income, if I retired there and then. It could not be done, so I just struggled on.

Between cancers one and two, I had travelled a lot. I had paid two more visits to Paris and been to Florence, Rapallo, Portofino, St Marguerite, Genoa and Pisa. After recovering from my second cancer, I went to Dinard, St Malo, Switzerland, Holland and Majorca—and later, when I was in my seventies, I toured France by car for three weeks with two friends.

We crossed by hovercraft from Ramsgate to Dover, staying the first and last nights of our tour at Arras. We had not intended going anywhere near Paris but somehow we found ourselves in the suburbs of that city. Our driver got out of the car to ask a policeman for directions and I took advantage of the stop to hop out also, run up and down the pavement and take a look in a shop window. My friends stared at me with amazement and asked what this was in aid of. I replied that when we returned home I could say that I had been to Paris—the friend who had remained seated in the car could make no such claim!

When the time came for my retirement, I received my presentation from the Principal and staff at a luncheon party in a hotel adjacent to the college. The usual speeches were made, each more flowery than the last, until I began to wonder who on earth they were talking about! I certainly did not recognise myself. One speech however gave me a great deal of satisfaction and that was when someone had, prior to the occasion, looked up the examination records and discovered that over the years I had had an average of between 90 and 100 per cent passes except in 1958, the year when I was off work for a time dealing with cancer number two. I was really thrilled to learn this—more so than with anything else which was said that day. My teaching career was finished and I was leaving the profession knowing that I had done my best for my students; I had equipped them each to earn their own living.

The scene when I said goodbye to my students was both emotional and tearful as each class in turn gave me a parting gift. The dress and jacket that I wore at the luncheon had been designed and made for me by my senior students. Could anything have been more fitting? Forgotten were all the scoldings I had given them over the years: forgotten also, the number of times I would not accept shoddy work from them and made them start at the beginning and do everything all over again!

Years later I received a letter from a student designing in London, who wrote that she did not know whether I was dead or alive but that when struggling to get some drapery right, she had suddenly thought that I would have known what to do! As I had come into her mind after an interval of some thirty years she decided to write to me, hoping that I was still alive for she wanted to tell me how much she appreciated all that I had done for her—how I had so often made her start again and seek in herself the best she could do.

In a subsequent letter she told me the following story, which I had forgotten. Evidently, she had come into the class one Monday morning and proudly told me that over the weekend she had made the blouse she was wearing. It seems that I glanced quickly at the blouse, admired it, praised the design and then told her that the collar was an eighth of an inch out on one side. She assured me that it could not be 'out', as she had carefully measured it and both sides were alike. I told her to measure it again, so there and then she took off the blouse and measured each side of the collar ... it was out by exactly an eighth of an inch. The girl said that no one would have noticed but me, and it appears that I replied that the two of us now knew that the collar was uneven and that unless she corrected it, every time she wore the blouse she would be conscious of the unevenness—and worse still, think that everyone else noticed it too and she would have no pleasure in wearing it!

7

A Reassurance

The New Year—1976—had just been born, thus allowing 1975 and my three-quarter century to pass into history. The old year ended, strangely enough, with a television variety programme covering seventy-five years of entertainment, starting with the beginning of the twentieth century when Queen Victoria was still on the throne, and ending with the singing of Auld Lang Syne. Medically, I should not really have been alive to watch the 1976 New Year in, but alive I was and so with a heart full of happiness I sang all the old songs at the top of my voice, along with the different impersonators of the old music-hall stars, just for the sheer joy and thankfulness of life.

1975 was a memorable and truly remarkable year for me. It was the year that I was told I had my fourth cancer, and before that year was over I was to hear the most amazing news, that my cancer was cured! I had expected and prepared for death but death did not come. In my story I have just got as far as my second cancer, but I wanted you to know my wonderful news before you go on to read about cancers three and four.

Now I'll go back in time again and restart where I left off—at cancer number two.

8

Celtic Art & A New Career

As I had always led a very busy life and had a keen interest in people and in things, my friends in England were concerned that when I retired I would be lonely, living—as they put it—'at the back of beyond' with nothing to occupy my time. To allay their fears, I brought home a large box of books, mostly thrillers, which had been partially collected for me by my friends. Would you believe it if I told you that life in the country is so hectic that I have only read about one third of the books that were in that box?

During the winter there is the Women's Guild—not, I hasten to add, the dull sewing meetings of a decade ago. In our Guild everyone talks; not small talk, but on subjects about which we feel strongly. We all air our views freely on anything from abortion to the problems of the young, the old, the state of the church and the nation, and there is never a needle in sight! In a nutshell, we are Women's Lib, from the oldest member to the youngest.

Then there is the Women's Institute with good speakers, demonstrators and the usual competitions. One society in which I have a special interest is the Mull Historical Society, of which I am a founder member. The preservation of our island history, its stories, legends and its rich heritage of Celtic art enthrals me.

As a student in Glasgow, most of my spare time was spent in the various libraries reading every book I could find that had any bearing on the Celtic people. I became obsessed with the subject, particularly Celtic art. As I was an art student at the time I suppose this was not to be wondered at. I made a special study of Celtic ornament: how the patterns were formed, and their relationship to other forms of ornament, tracing the origins of the patterns from before the La Tène period through the Early Christian period and on to the twelfth century, when this form of art had reached its peak and before it became debased. This great interest of mine latterly extended to include Celtic women, their unique talents and their art secrets, which the great Caesar himself said were unknown to the women of other nations. He even remarked on their great beauty. Can you wonder that as a woman, I was interested?

One result of this was that I wrote articles for the press, both on Celtic art and on Celtic women. The follow-up of the articles resulted in invitations to speak on the subject to various societies up and down the country. When talking about Celtic art, I found that you could hold an audience and take them along with you by demonstrating how the patterns came to be evolved. Watching a pattern developing on a blackboard before their eyes kept the interest of the audience throughout.

The first talk I ever gave was to the Glasgow branch of the Scottish Ecclesiological Society. I was young, and was naturally nervous talking to such an august body. So I asked my sister to come and sit in the audience and listen to any remarks made, and to tell me about them afterwards. This would make sure that should I ever be asked to speak again, I would know the pitfalls to avoid. Above all, I wanted to know if my voice carried without strain: that is, my usual speaking voice.

The talk was in the afternoon, in a church hall. The lectern stood immediately in front of a stained-glass window in which there was a round portion, and it so happened that the round part made a sort of frame for my head. My sister told me that the two ladies sitting behind her remarked, one to the other, 'Isn't she beautiful!' She turned round to see who they were talking about and discovered that they were looking at me (but were wearing glasses with thick lenses!) Then my sister had another look at me and realised that the afternoon sun was shining through the coloured glass in the window and that the circle appeared like a halo around my head! Well, if you want to come down to earth, ask your sister what you look like. No, she could not tell me how my talk went because she had heard me rehearse it at home and so had not listened, and anyhow she was used to the sound of my voice, so to her it carried!

At this time, the *Glasgow Evening Times* had a column entitled 'Gossip and Grumbles'. I knew that my talk was a success when the following statement appeared in the next edition:

> The Celts, says a lecturer, excelled in illumination; some of their fans, however, would prefer to see some of them throwing more light on goal-scoring.

I had arrived! To be mentioned in the 'Gossip and Grumbles' was indeed an honour, even if it was related to a football team!

A year later I gave a talk to the Edinburgh branch of the same society, which was held in St Cuthbert's Halls. After the talk, an old gentleman introduced himself to me and said that he was John Duncan, the artist. He told me that I, a 'mere slip of a girl', had done something that he, a much older man, would never have had the courage to do. On being asked what that was he replied, 'Do freehand drawings in front of so many people.' I told him that for me it was a relief to turn my back on all those people, for while I was doing the drawings I could forget them! I had never met John Duncan before but had always admired his work, particularly his stained-glass window in Paisley Abbey.

Although retired, I was determined to use my brain to the utmost, presenting myself with problems that had to be solved—thus making sure that my thinking did not deteriorate through boredom. Therefore, knowing the Scottish Education Department had started the Scottish Certificate of Education at A and O level in general design and in dress design, I applied to be considered as an examiner. I had all the qualifications required and I knew that I could do the job with competence, having taken my students in England to National Diploma level. I was accepted and so started a new career which lasted for the duration of one month each year, for eight years.

The examination work, from all over Scotland, was sent by the schools to Edinburgh to be marked. The marking process impressed me very much as I was now seeing things, as it were, from the other side of the coin.

That first year, 1961, the examiners were: six HM Inspectors, three retired heads of departments and two teaching heads of departments. The procedure was that we each marked the work of three pupils, then we passed our three on to another examiner who in turn passed it to an HM Inspector. We then discussed the marks and so arrived at a uniform standard. The surprising thing was that our marking never varied more than half a mark to one and a half marks at the outside, between different examiners. Often when we came to a borderline case we would re-mark it, looking for an extra half mark somewhere. It was then given to another examiner to mark, and discussed point by point until we agreed. If only the failed pupil could have seen how painstakingly this was done!

I continued as an examiner until cancer number three appeared, when I regretfully had to give the job up. I had thoroughly enjoyed carrying on my old work from a new angle, meeting Scottish heads of departments and comparing teaching methods in Scotland and England. The methods were similar as, also, were the results.

9

Cancer Number Three

On arrival home after retirement one of the first things I did was to take a long, hard look at my house and view it with a 'seeing' eye, and not just with the nostalgic eye of looking at 'home'. As my house is one of the first that a visitor sees on arrival in Salen, I decided to make the outside appearance as attractive as possible. So I got several lorry loads of seashore gravel to spread over the ground between the house and the edge of the road. Arranged at intervals of three feet apart, I made rose beds along the front of the house and planted pansies around each rose bush. Then, where the gravel and the road met, I planted aubrietia and other border plants, which were in flower for about eight months out of the twelve so I was truly delighted with the results. I was less pleased with the daffodil bulbs I planted on the other side of the road, opposite the house, for no sooner had a yellow head appeared in the spring than some child, thinking it was wild, picked it! I have now replaced the bulbs with shrubs. Looking back, I am surprised that it never entered my head that I might not live to see the fruits of my labour, having two cancers behind me!

My case history had been transferred from England to the radiotherapy department of a Glasgow hospital, and it was to this hospital that I went when my annual check-up was due.

In September 1969 I went as usual, expecting to be told that everything was all right. I was so sure that all was well that I had even booked a flight to Guernsey for the day following the check-up, to pay a visit to my sister and her husband. On this occasion the doctor who examined me seemed to take a long time feeling around one area of my only breast. I asked if there was anything wrong and was told that he would need a second opinion and not to re-dress until he returned with a consultant. I waited, alone, for about an hour—one of the longest hours of my life.

When the doctor returned he brought a surgeon with him and the surgeon confirmed what the doctor had suspected, that I had a lump in my other breast. I use the word 'in', for the lump was not visible; I did not know it was there and I had no pain. After we had a talk about it, I told the surgeon that I would like the lump removed as soon as possible and he said that he also would like it removed without delay, and asked when could I enter hospital for the operation. I replied 'Immediately', and so it was fixed that I would go in to hospital and be operated on within the next couple of days. On being asked who would perform the operation, he replied that he would. I looked straight into his eyes and in that one look I knew that here was a man who had integrity, who would do his best for any patient—a man I could trust. I knew nothing about him, nothing of his skill as a surgeon, but he gave me the confidence that every patient who is facing an operation needs.

I had no clothes suitable for hospital wear, so after the consultation I went out and bought a couple of bed jackets and wrote a note to my niece Sheila in Salen, and asked her to open up my house and post me some extra nightdresses. When I arrived home and told my sister-in-law my news, I think she was more shocked than I was, for I suppose deep down there had always lurked at the back of my mind the thought that one day at a check-up I would be told that I had a new cancer. Had I not been a bit stunned with this news I think I would have laughed, for over the years I had spent hours and hours trying to perfect the artificial breast to look normal, and now I had been told that I was to lose the other breast. The compensation would be that when all was over, both sides would be matching!

All went well during and after the operation, until the pathologist's report came through.

I remember it so well.

I was sitting up in bed one evening having my tea when I saw my surgeon enter the ward and make for my bed. I knew by his face what he had come to say, even before he had reached my bedside. He told me that he had just received the pathologist's report, and that my third cancer was again a primary, but that this new one had travelled. I think at that moment I was more sorry for the surgeon having to give me this news than I was for myself. I did not ask him how far the new cancer had travelled; it was enough to know that it had travelled, and I knew just what that meant.

The consultant told me that I would require radiotherapy and would therefore remain a patient in the same ward while I was having the treatment. He stayed with me for a wee while and talked to me. I told him that I had stood up to being told I had cancer twice before in my life and that I could stand the knowledge again. Then he left me to my thoughts. Strange how we get strength, from we know not where, when we need it—possibly the spirit within us taking over the physical part of us and making the physical numb. I cannot remember finishing my tea or what it consisted of ... I knew that I was being tested yet again and I prayed that I might not fail.

By a strange quirk of fate there happened to be another woman in the ward who had to have her breast removed, and this poor woman was in such a state of fear of the unknown that the sister asked me to have a word with her to allay her fears. I sat with her for some time, told her that I had had my breast removed twenty years previously and was still alive to tell that tale, that she had nothing to worry about, just to trust in God and in the skill of the surgeon and she would be all right. She never shed another tear and went off to the theatre quite calm. Her tumour turned out to be non-malignant; mine was malignant but fortunately that woman only knew about her own condition and not mine.

When the radiologist came to see me it was arranged that I should go to her department to be 'marked out' at a given time, in a day or two. This was an interesting experience and in many respects resembled the procedure when I first visited a radiologist almost two decades earlier. I was put lying on a table while my chest, back, neck and side were marked with a blue pencil, and I was told not to wash it off. Further, I was advised that while I was having the treatment, no water must come in contact with the skin of the affected part.

The radiologist was a delightful woman, and was most interested in seeing the results on my skin of the radiotherapy treatment I had received so many years ago. She told me that radiotherapy had made rapid advances since that first time in 1950, and that after the exposures this time my skin would look quite normal—a little darker in colour perhaps, just like sunburn that was wearing off. She explained to me that six or seven beams from the machine would be directed from different positions, all aiming at the same area. The treatments were to be daily, except weekends, and there would be about fifteen or twenty in all.

This time I was less afraid; I had been through it all once before so I knew more or less what to expect. While I was being prepared I was more relaxed than I had been twenty years earlier, so I was able to have a good look around me and take in what I saw.

The huge machine occupied the greater part of the room and was in some ways different to the first one. Instead of the extended arm being moved over my body to the required position as I lay on the table, when the 'packing' stage was completed the table was moved under the arm of the machine. I also noticed that at the end of the arm there was a square fixture, possibly made of Perspex, through which the beam would come. The size of this fixture was changed to suit the size of the area where the beam was wanted.

The massive door was then closed and I was left alone lying there, almost afraid to breathe lest I altered my position but remaining just as steady as a rock. My eyes, however, could observe what was directly in front of me. It was comforting to see the little window through which I was being checked. I learned afterwards that the machine was German and was the latest model. When alone in the room I could hear the sound of water as well as the hum from the machine. This intrigued me, for no water was visible, nor could I see a water container. One day I asked about it and was told that water was required for this machine; how it was used I do not know.

During the four weeks of my treatment I had a blood sample taken every day—I wondered why, so I asked! I was told that it was essential in order to make sure that the balance between the white and red corpuscles did not alter. One day I asked the girl taking the blood if she needed to take such a big sample, would a smaller one not do? I was bloodless and could not afford to lose much. She laughed and said that she understood my anxiety and would be careful to take the exact amount required, no more and no less—and she would not spill a drop. I was reminded of Portia and Shylock in the Merchant of Venice!

I was nauseated every day that I had the treatment, with the sickness starting about five hours later. Immediately after the treatment, I was put to bed as soon as I returned to the ward. Everyone was so very kind to me, even the tea lady made me a special cup of tea when I got back into bed. I was given pills to combat the sickness, and I am sure that they helped but I felt really ill for the whole of the period I was having the radiotherapy. So ill in fact, that I do not think that my spirits could have been lower. One night, sleepless and nauseous, I suddenly realised that I was feeling very sorry for myself, and felt ashamed. Ashamed because I knew that I had no need to be sorry for myself—God was beside me, everyone was doing their best for me, and I was still alive. I would need to snap out of it.

Then I thought of how ashamed of me my mother would have been, she who had taught me to face life with courage, bravely. Now, my mother, a native Gaelic speaker, often used a phrase when she felt ashamed of herself (for reasons which appeared to us her children as simply ridiculous). She would use this phrase if an unexpected guest arrived and her first thoughts would be, had she enough in the house to give her guest to eat? It was a standing joke in the family, for the table was always generously laden with plenty to spare for several more guests, had they come. The phrase was *Mo Naire*, which translated means, 'my shame'—or simply, 'I'm ashamed of myself': for hospitality to a Highlander is a sacred duty. On this particular night in hospital, when I was at my lowest spiritually, I kept repeating to myself, '*Mo Naire*'. I felt that if I stopped, I would lose hope and die. Then I wrote the following lines:

> Mo Naire, that I afraid should be—with the Lord my
> God so close to me
> Mo Naire, that I but darkness see—with the light of
> Heaven encircling me

I knew that night what it was like to reach the depths. I knew also that one has to reach the depths before one can rise to the heights. There had been moments that night when I had lacked faith, and faith together with prayer had always upheld me. I knew, too, that to wallow in self-pity was an insult to God who had given me life to be lived. Do you wonder at my cry from the heart, *Mo Naire*?

When I was allowed out of hospital I was told that I would have a severe burning feeling in my skin and that I had to report back to hospital every second day, so that they could keep an eye on the skin and make sure it did not 'break'. Meanwhile, I was given a quantity of gentian with which to paint the affected parts and gauze with which to apply it.

I was staying with Sadie, who apart from being my sister-in-law, had been my close friend for over fifty years. We had shared together both joys and sorrows, and more, she had shared her children with me—Sheila, Angus and Fiona—so it fell to Sadie to apply the gentian. This she tenderly did, morning, noon and evening, and often during the night when I walked the floor with burn pains that were almost unbearable. Sadie, when she was not making me cups of tea, walked the floor with me, with the gentian bottle in one hand and an orange stick wrapped around with gauze in the other. Then one morning, when I returned to hospital, the sister looked at my face and remarked that I had had a bad night from the look of me. I told her that I hoped I would not have to stand many more like it. She checked the dates on my case sheet, then the calendar, and said that the burning was at its height now and that it would gradually lessen. And lessen it did.

That was cancer number three. Well, I thought to myself, here we go again! All through my life when things went wrong (and my goodness, how often they did!)—when, metaphorically speaking, I was flat on my face—I had just picked myself up, dusted myself down, dried my tears and started life all over again.

In short, I never knew when I was beaten! I do not know whether you would consider this a vice or a virtue, I've often wondered myself. All I know was that I had to face life bravely no matter what the odds, and the odds were that I had never known or heard of anyone surviving three cancers over a period of twenty years. I went about repeating to myself, '*Audentes Fortuna Juvat*' (Fortune favours the brave), my mother's clan motto—and I could not think of a better one.

Things could be worse ... I was still alive, mobile, no signs of senility so far, and my seventieth birthday was just around the corner: my allotted span of threescore years and ten. My form of cancer was not the worst kind, I told myself—mine was just within the human frame and although malignant, would only destroy myself. The worst kind of cancer to my way of thinking was man-made. It lived in the mind, fed on jealousy and possessiveness, ate away the heart, and destroyed both the 'host' and the happiness of other people—a truly malignant cancer.

Nothing lasts for ever, and soon I was back home on Mull, in my own house and in my own bed. That night I thanked God for the sheer wonder of my life, vowed that I would do my best to be worthy of the 'bonus' days and perhaps years, and use each day to the full.

10

Making Wine

When I got my strength back, I looked about for new interests ... and so started to make wine! Now wine takes time to mature, and with a third cancer just behind me and not knowing what was in front of me, you might think that this was a bit daft and I agree with you. I might never live to drink the wine but someone else would and so I would make 'good' wine.

I chose the hedgerow flowers first, for the flowers cost nothing, they just needed picking—and what could be nicer than picking sweet-smelling mayflower? Over the next six years I made gallons of elderflower, mayflower, parsley, barley, raspberry, gooseberry, plum, apple and banana wines. What fun I had with my winemaking! To begin with, I used too much yeast, which resulted in an overflow of froth running down the sides of the jar and covering a good part of the floor. When the frothing had ceased, airlock corks had to be put in the jars and the jars placed in front of the fire in the dining room. My problems were just about to begin.

First, I had to keep the wine at an even temperature, no easy task in an old house! If the wind veered round to the north-west, a draught came under the door, through ill-fitting window frames, even through the keyhole! So, early in the evening, folded newspapers had to be jammed between the door and the jamb, another stuck in the keyhole, and for good measure I hung a travelling rug over a clothes-maid which enclosed three sides of the wine jars. The fourth side was exposed to the fire. My own warmth had to take second place to the wine and so I sat with one leg and foot exposed to the fire while the other leg, and the rest of me, was wrapped in rugs. The leg exposed to the fire developed an unsightly mottled appearance on the skin, a condition we call in Gaelic *breacan*, meaning 'tartan'—a word used by the Celts from the earliest times to describe a garment of many colours, worn like a cloak. Come to think of it, Joseph's coat of many colours could have been tartan. Well, my one leg had all seven colours of the rainbow!

After three months the wine had to be racked, thus leaving the lees at the bottom of the jar and the clear wine syphoned into a clean one. This part was best done by two people, so for this operation I enlisted the help of my niece Sheila. Now the first mouthful of wine, you are expected to spit out, as the wine is not ready for drinking; but more often than not we forgot, or it just slipped down our throats without our noticing. Anyhow, by the end of a syphoning session we were both merry, full of heartburn from the new wine—yes, decidedly merry! Anyone who tells you that home-made wine is an insipid beverage ... take this information with a pinch of salt. Sheila and I would have laughed at our shadows, and we sang for the sheer joy of being alive. I cannot think of anything more therapeutic than a good laugh—and many a good laugh we did have!

During this time, between cancers three and four, I had to return to the hospital for regular check-ups every two months to begin with, then every three months, gradually working up to two visits a year.

When I returned home after the last radiotherapy treatment I saw quite a lot of my own doctor, to whose care, attention and encouragement I owe much. I was able to talk to him freely and I knew that any question I asked him would be answered truthfully. While having a discussion with him one day I asked him how long it would be, assuming the radiotherapy had not arrested the travelling cancer, before a secondary appeared. He told me anything from two to five years, as cancer travels slower the older one is—perhaps never, as old age might take over. I had not previously thought about my trouble in relation to my age but now I did and I rejoiced in my threescore years and ten! I asked him where in the body a secondary would be likely to appear and I was told in one of three places, in all probability: the brain, the spine or the pelvis. I told him sincerely that I hoped it would not be the brain, as I would like to have a clear brain right up to the very end. I remember so well how he patted my arm reassuringly and said that if there was a secondary, it would appear in about five years and that by then I would be seventy-five, and seventy-five years was a good age! Anyhow he said that he believed I would die of old age.

11

Painting & Decorating

Well, there was no use standing idly by waiting for old age to catch up with me, so I decided to redecorate the inside of the house. This was a job that would keep me busy over a fairly long period; there was just one snag—I had never hung wallpaper before, but I had once seen a film showing the correct way to do it and I thought that I could remember. Anyhow, I would have a go.

I did my bedroom first, thinking that if I made mistakes no one would see them but myself. The finished job was not too bad: just a few creases here and there which were not very noticeable. By the time I had finished papering the third bedroom I had improved so much that I had enough confidence to tackle the dining room. This room has fairly heavy furniture and large oil paintings, including portraits, so I had nothing to worry about. With any luck the furniture and the pictures would help to cover up my mistakes. I left the lounge to the last, for here mistakes would show—so I bought wallpaper that did not need matching, and hoped for the best.

My success as a painter and decorator must have gone to my head for I had no sooner finished the lounge than I decided to paint the inside of the porch, and it was here that I thought I had met my Waterloo. I knew before I started that I should not attempt this job for it meant working above my head, painting the ceiling. However, I've always had a lot of imagination, and before I had put a brush into the paint pot I visualised the finished work with gleaming white paint, a well-polished table, shining brasses and lovely green pot plants. With this picture at the back of my mind I made an enthusiastic start, but I'm sorry to say my enthusiasm evaporated before the end of the first day. Having started, I had to finish—which I eventually did at the end of the third day. Too tired to do my washing-up after the evening meal, I relaxed in front of the television screen.

When the programme I had been watching finished, I went into the kitchenette to wash the dishes. As I looked through the window which overlooks my half acre of wilderness once called a garden, I saw a beautiful stag about twenty yards from the house.

I quietly returned to the dining room, sat down, tried not to feel alarmed, closed my eyes and gave myself a good scolding. I told myself that I was seeing things that were not there. I had no right to work above my head for I now carried mirrored in my eyes the vision of the stag's head which hung on the wall of the porch. After a few minutes I plucked up the courage to open my eyes and, moving my head very slowly, looked around the room.

Taking comfort in the fact that the sideboard, table and chairs were in their usual places and not a stag in sight, I ventured back into the kitchenette. Sure enough, there was the stag—large as life and not just a head; and this time he was accompanied by two hinds!

I dashed out of the front door to my nearest neighbour, who was working in his garden, and asked him to come quickly and tell me if I was seeing things; I was so sure I was having hallucinations! The neighbour came running, not knowing what I wanted him to see, looked out and said, 'You have a beautiful stag there and two lovely hinds.' What a relief for me!

That stag was a real beauty, with a wonderful head of antlers. At about the same time every evening for three weeks or so the stag and his hinds returned, and what pleasure they gave to me, observing them at such close quarters.

Of course, in between the papering and painting there was always the vegetable plot to attend to, and the never-ending job of weeding the gravel and the drive. I made a point of having an annual holiday every September after my check-up, when I visited friends and relations in the Channel Islands and scattered all over England. Twice I had a spring holiday—once to Scarborough and once to Blackpool. The Scarborough holiday was chosen because of its close proximity to York, a city I had always wanted to explore, and this you will understand ... but you might ask yourself or me, why Blackpool with its Golden Mile, glittering lights and cheerful shows?

The answer is simple: Blackpool was the only place I could think of that was as unlike Mull as it could possibly be. The familiar can dull our senses to the people and things around us until we do not really see or appreciate them. Only by looking at a different scene do we truly observe the scene around us and see it through new eyes.

12

Cancer Number Four

In the spring of 1975 I had not been feeling too well. I had suffered a bout of flu and had arthritis in my back and a general feeling of being run down. More, for some reason I could not account for, I had a conviction that things were not quite right with my pelvis. I did tell my doctor, but there was nothing I could put my finger on, and how does one explain a conviction without proof? However, the doctor said that when I next went to see the consultant he would give me a letter to take to him and the consultant would, if he deemed it necessary, have my back x-rayed.

When I saw the consultant in March he arranged that I should be x-rayed from head to toe. Now, I would like you to remember March—the third month of that year—for it is a vitally important month in the calendar of events. When the x-rays were taken, I was told to return to my Glasgow address and to remain there until the results were known. That was on a Thursday. On the following

Tuesday, the phone rang and the call was for me. The consultant himself spoke to me and said that he was very sorry to have to tell me that I had a new cancer, several in fact, in a cluster in the pelvis. This very busy man had not delegated to one of his juniors the distasteful job of conveying bad news; he had elected to break it to me himself, and he did it very gently and his doing so gave me heart, if you know what I mean.

He asked me how soon I could get home to Mull, as he wanted me to start on a powerful drug straight away, and speed was important. My own doctor would prescribe the drug; meanwhile, I had to write down the name of the medication, the strength of each pill and the number of pills he wanted me to take daily. This verbal information was necessary because of the possible delay in the post. I told the consultant I could be on the evening train to Oban, where I could stay the night and be on the first boat to Mull the following morning, and so be at the doctor's surgery in time for his morning session. (This I did). I was then told I had to report back to the hospital in four weeks, by which time the consultant would know whether the drug was going to work or not. If not, I had to be prepared for more radiotherapy.

When I had cancer number three, I had thought I could not possibly survive for longer than a short period at most, in spite of my own doctor telling me that I should have five years—but survive I did. It had been five and a half years and the secondary cancer, as predicted, was in my pelvis. I thanked God it was not in the brain. As it was a fourth cancer, and inoperable, I felt sure

I could not survive this one. That this indeed was the end I was certain, and so I set about putting my affairs in order.

I had made my will almost thirty years previously, so that was all right. I knew that when I died my assets would be frozen until probate was granted to my two nieces, who were my joint heirs and executrices, so I had to make provision for them both to have some money to deal with immediate expenses. I wrote to the bank manager, explained the position and asked for his advice, suggesting that I should withdraw £300 or so from my account and divide this amount between Sheila and Fiona. Then if I died in a Glasgow hospital, Fiona—who lived in Glasgow—would have some money to hand to deal with immediate expenses. Sheila, in Oban, would have the same amount should she need to pay for anything at the Oban or Mull end. The bank manager was most helpful, fully realised the position and advised me that as both nieces were joint heirs, the best thing to do was to take out two mandate forms, one for each niece, then they could both be issued with cheque-books and be able to withdraw money from my account as required. This was a great relief to me, and a weight was lifted from my shoulders. Fortunately, I trusted both nieces implicitly and knew that they would carry out my wishes to the best of their ability.

When passing through Oban before my check-up, I had bought some beautiful tweed material to make a coat and skirt for myself. I also bought seeds for my vegetable plot. So, not wanting to waste the seeds, or for that matter to sit down and await death, I decided to plant them.

Preparing the ground was hard work and the arthritis in my back did not help any, so I did no digging, just worked the ground over with a fork and got rid of the weeds. Sometimes I worked for an hour, went indoors, put a tablespoonful of brandy or whisky in a cup of coffee to which I had added a generous amount of sugar, sat down and drank it. When another hour had passed I had renewed my strength and went back to my task on the vegetable patch. When the ground was raked over, shallow drills made with the back of the rake and the seeds sown, I hopefully left the rest to nature, believing that if I did not live to eat the vegetables when they were mature, well, someone else would.

At the end of the four-week period I returned to Glasgow to keep my appointment with the consultant, fully prepared for radiotherapy. When the consultant asked me if I had any pain, he seemed surprised when I told him that I had no pain other than my usual arthritis. He told me there was a possibility that the drug was going to be effective and that he would be in a better position to tell me in another four weeks, when he wanted to see me again. Meanwhile he would postpone the decision about radiotherapy until my next visit, which was fixed for mid-May.

Back I went to Mull and at this time, mid-April, the spring sunshine showed up the havoc of the winter on indoor paintwork, curtains and so on. So between April and May I kept myself busy doing some spring cleaning, a little at a time, until I had the place spick and span with all the curtains and cushion covers laundered. What a blessing was bestowed on the world by the man who invented the washing machine and spin drier!

During the period between March and May, I went over all my papers and burnt old letters. I even found old love letters and was surprised that I could not recall the sender! That little lot was the first to be consumed by the flames, for the romance could not have been the 'Romeo and Juliet' type when it made no lasting impression on me!

At my mid-May check-up I was again asked if I had any pain, and again I said that I had not. This time, the consultant said he was now sure that the drug was proving effective and he thought I would not need radiotherapy, but to report back to him in mid-June. After the check-up I returned to Mull with a much lighter heart but afraid to be too optimistic.

I had another look at the coat material I had bought in March, thought it a pity not to put it to some use, and as neither of my nieces were inclined towards dressmaking and as the material had been expensive, I decided to make it up for myself. I reasoned it out like this: I still had no pain, and I knew that severe pain with cancer comes at the end. Cancer travels slowly with age, and I was seventy-five; a new garment would give a boost to my morale—also, I had to be kept busy. So, I made a coat and skirt and very nice they look!

13

Bed & Breakfast

One evening, a Dutch couple came to the door looking for somewhere to stay for the night, just for bed and breakfast. They said they had tried everywhere without success and they had no idea where they were going to lay their heads that night. I could see the wife was pregnant and I suddenly thought of Mary, Joseph and the Christ Child, and on the spur of the moment said I had spare rooms and would put them up for the night.

After having dinner at the local hotel, they returned and together we spent a happy and most interesting evening around a cheery fire. They told me something about the life and customs of the Dutch and I told them old Hebridean stories, so you could say 'a good time was had by all'.

That started me in the bed and breakfast business! I so thoroughly enjoyed the company of the Dutch couple, and found their conversation so stimulating, that I wondered why I had not thought of bed and breakfast guests before. Not every night—which would have been too tiring for me—but perhaps once or twice a week, as an interest and because in any case, I like people!

I had guests from Sweden, Germany, Norway and of course, England. They all, without exception, helped with the washing-up after breakfast, made their own beds, and best of all, gave me their company in the evening after they returned from the hotel where they had dinner. Our evenings were spent talking, interspersed with tea, cakes and biscuits, or home-made wine, and our talk often went on until after midnight! They said coming into a private house made their holiday. What none of them knew was that their presence in my home at this particular time was very therapeutic for me. I felt that God intended me to have companionship during this very worrying and trying period in my life.

My mid-June check-up was again satisfactory, and another appointment was made for me for mid-July. By this time I began to feel that I had bought a part of the bus, boat and railway! In July, the consultant confirmed that obviously the drug was working for me, and that I could now miss a month and return in September. In September he intended to have me x-rayed, then he would compare the new x-rays with those taken in March and so see if the cluster of cancers in the pelvis had travelled. He told me he felt fairly confident that the spread had been arrested otherwise I would not now be feeling as well as I was, with still no pain. It was at this consultation that I was told that in March I had not just one cluster of cancers in the pelvis, but several. Whether one cluster or several, it was still cancer for the fourth time and I could not see how anyone could survive. Death, I felt, was just being delayed and must surely come ere long.

Once again I was back on Mull and living a life as normal as possible, continuing with my paying guests and other activities. During August I adjudicated at two agricultural shows—in the art, craft and needlework sections of both. To adjudicate at any local competition is the equivalent of standing in front of a firing squad! Everyone goes round the stalls afterwards doing their own judging, asking anyone who happens to be near why so-and-so did not get a prize for this or that, when the craftsmanship was superior to the article awarded the prize. In this I often agreed, but 'so-and-so' had not read the schedule properly and I had to adjudicate according to the schedule. Because of this, many excellent specimens were disqualified. I used to wonder if it was safe to go home afterwards, or wiser to emigrate!

14

Consolation

We all at some time in our lives give a passing thought to death and the hereafter, particularly when we suffer a bereavement. In the fullness of life, the subject is regarded as either morbid or distasteful and so we conveniently forget it.

All primitive people were sun-worshippers. The Egyptians in their hieroglyphics portrayed the Sun God in a boat taking the souls of the dead to—I know not where. Nearer home, the Druids had their own sun worship with the summer solstice. For me it was a single sunbeam, creating a heaven of my own here on earth. This was the way of it ...

One winter morning in St Columba's Parish Church, Glasgow, I was sitting in our usual pew on the east side of the central aisle, when out of the grey gloom there came a sunbeam through one of the east windows. It seemed to rest on me, then as the sun moved in the sky, the sunbeam appeared to travel down the central aisle until it halted at the communion table. If my thoughts had been wandering during the service, I became suddenly alert as it flashed into my mind that with the sunbeam, Christ had entered His house! Imagination? What else?

Later, when I found myself alone in the home that had known the laughter of children and wherein had always dwelt love and a peacefulness I cannot put into words, I was to remember my sunbeam. I remembered it when the sun streamed through the dining room window, first resting on the sideboard then slowly filling the entire room. I got—and still get—the feeling that God has come into the house, blessing me and everyone under my roof, sitting at my table and sharing my meal.

A single sunbeam came to mean God, life, death and the hereafter to me and with it the fear of death vanished. I suppose in a way at this period of my life I was living almost with death daily, and I could not just shove it aside and forget it.

One day, when death does come, I hope my soul will take the golden path from the seashore to the mystical, imaginary island in the west which appears at sunset and disappears when the sun dips into the sea on the horizon. This island, *Tir Nan Og*—the land of the ever-young—is only visible to the discerning eye and that eye, Celtic.

15

Cure

I suppose that all powerful drugs have some side effects, and while I was prepared for this, and did have several, there was one which I was not prepared for. I found that I was undergoing a physiognomy change!

I had been sewing and noticed what I took to be a dark thread falling over my face from my forehead which, when brushed aside, kept falling back again. At last I caught it between finger and thumb and pulled, only to discover it was attached to my head. Still holding it, I walked over to the mirror and found that it was a dark hair, several dark hairs in fact. Not believing my eyes, I fluffed up my hair all around and sure enough—my white hair was streaked with brown. In short, my hair was changing back to its original colour.

My grand-niece Fiona, who is very concerned about my 'looks', had given me a skin moisturiser for my birthday, so when the tone of my skin improved I put it down to the moisturiser ... but when the brown age spots started to disappear, I began to wonder! However, I did have other things on my mind so I did not dwell on my facial appearance.

It was only on my next visit to Oban when Sheila remarked that my wrinkles were less noticeable that I went upstairs, put on my glasses and studied myself in the mirror. My face did look less aged! Here I was, with a drug that was not only curing my cancer but was giving me rejuvenation treatment at the same time. I felt that my rejuvenation was complete when, while I was out shopping with my niece Sheila and grand-nephew Glenn and preceding them by a yard or two, the boy turned to his mother and said, 'Look at Aunty—you would think she was twenty-four years old if only she had platform shoes.'

No, I did not dash to buy platform shoes; to tell you the truth, I didn't know whether to laugh or cry. The difference between twenty-four and seventy-five vanishes when you are seen through the loving eyes of a ten-year-old boy, a very manly boy, tugging at the heartstrings and making you feel twenty-four years old all over again!

In September I told the consultant that I felt so well I was afraid that I was a fraud, taking up so much of his time. I was again x-rayed from head to toe and told to stay on in Glasgow until the consultant had received the x-ray plates and had the time to study them. He told me he would phone the results to me, possibly in a few days. Now my check-up was on a Thursday, as usual, so I did not really expect to hear anything before the following Tuesday.

However, on the Monday morning the phone rang and I answered it myself. The caller was none other than the consultant, to say he had the most wonderful news for me: my pelvic bones were back to normal and my fourth cancer was cured! He sounded so pleased that he kept repeating, several times, 'It is amazing!'

I could not at first take it in; I had expected death and I had prepared myself for death, and now to be told this very wonderful news. Well, how would you have felt? What would you have said or done? I told the consultant that had he been at my end of the phone, I would have hugged him—I never gave a thought to medical etiquette! Then what did I do? I did something I had never done when I had been told I had cancer for the first, second, third or fourth time—I put down the phone and wept! I had never shed a tear because I had cancer; never asked myself resentfully why it had to happen to me, not once but four times. I had just accepted it. It was my cross and it had to be borne. Now, all the pent-up feelings of a quarter of a century erupted and the tears cascaded down my cheeks. How did I feel? My feelings are difficult to describe and I do not think I can describe them adequately, so I leave that to your imagination.

I hugged my sister-in-law, who just wept with me tears of relief and pure joy. I do not remember what we said to each other but I remember laughing in the midst of our tears and drinking cups of tea without even noticing or counting the number of cups we drank! What a strange thing joy is, and stranger still that joy and sorrow affect us identically, both bringing the emotions from our inmost depth to the surface where they cease to be twins, separate and take on a new identity—the one of gratitude and the other of resentment.

When I had recovered sufficiently I went into town, called at the BEA office and booked a flight to the Isle of Man. If I had had my passport with me I would have made it to Rome, a city I long to see; however my passport was at home in Mull so I settled for the Isle of Man, where I had never been. It was a spur of the moment decision and the booking clerk, on hearing this, asked me if I had booked accommodation on the island. Discovering that I had not, he looked at me in a pitying way, picked up the phone and got through to the Isle of Man Tourist Board, who made a reservation for me at a hotel. I told the booking clerk I wanted to travel immediately, so I was on the first flight the following day.

When I arrived at Douglas I phoned the hotel, and the proprietor said to wait at the air-bus terminal and his wife, driving a red Mini, would collect me. To avoid confusion, I described myself to him as of middle age(!) and told him what I was wearing.

At the hotel, a pot of tea and a plate of sandwiches were awaiting me in the bar-lounge. What a lovely welcome to a lone stranger! At dinner that night, I found myself at a table for six. On my right, facing each other, was a middle-aged couple from Liverpool. I asked their names and 'Mrs' replied, 'I'm Hilda and this is Dave.' The young lady on my left said, 'I'm Maureen and this is my mother,' and the man directly opposite me told us his name was Tommy. I said, 'I'm Mairi.' So, I never even knew their surnames!

It turned out that we were all celebrating something. Dave had just retired, so he and Hilda were having the holiday they had always dreamt about and looked forward to for a very long time. Maureen had brought her mother to the Isle of Man from Belfast to get some respite from the bombing, and Tommy said he had also come from Ireland, for the same reason. We were all in the right mood to enjoy ourselves, and became friends from the word go.

When I was asked why I was visiting the Isle of Man, and alone too, I did not wish them to know the real reason; so I said that I was getting on in years and I had searched all over Scotland, England and Wales for a man, but without success. I had suddenly realised that I had been looking in the wrong places—the obvious place to look was the Isle of Man, and I was alone because I did not want competition!

Maureen found a boyfriend with whom she went dancing or to the casino at night, leaving 'mother' with me. At breakfast every morning she brought us up to date with the progress of her romance. I suspect that a great deal of the romance was invented for our entertainment—and most entertaining it was.

The day after my arrival, I went along to the Tourist Board to thank them for fixing me up in such a comfortable hotel. I was told that as a senior citizen I could if I liked pay £1, and be given a ticket which would entitle me to free travel on any bus or horse-drawn tram during the whole length of my stay on the island. The horse-drawn trams fascinated me, and as the arthritis in my back prevented me from doing much walking, I spent most of my time on them. I would get on to one tram, travel the whole length of the promenade, get off, board the next tram, and travel back to the other end.

On the first day it was pouring with rain and blowing a gale so I had the open-sided trams to myself. I was completely alone, radiantly happy, with a heart that sang for the sheer joy of being alive in this wonderful, wonderful world. I hope that you, the reader, will experience this kind of joy one day. I thanked God for every drop of rain that fell on me that day; each raindrop was like a blessing falling on my face straight from Heaven.

I had faced death with each cancer, and in facing it perhaps, learned something about the true meaning of life: that joy without suffering has no meaning, and only when the two fuse and become one do we really live and accept both life and death as part of existence—the one complementary to the other.

I felt an initial reluctance to write about my life, living with cancer. I thought it would be too painful reliving it all over again, but this has not been so. As a painting only comes to life when shade is added to the bright tones, so in retrospect, the dark patches in my life have been amply compensated by the bright ones.

Amazing Grace!

Afterword

'Amazing Grace' most of you will think of as a hit tune that stayed at the top of the pop charts for as long, or perhaps longer, than any other disc. The pipes at any time stir the blood, particularly if the blood is Highland and the tune that of an old Scottish psalm. Combine that with the words and your heart will melt with emotion. Mine does, but then for me 'Amazing Grace time' means a quarter-century bonus of life, twenty-five years or so crammed full of the love and understanding of family and friends, two and a half decades for which to thank God.

After cancer number three, I often wondered why I was still alive. In my heart I knew that I was alive because God had a purpose for me here on earth, and although I might never know what that purpose was, here I would stay until it was accomplished.

After cancer number four, I felt I knew what this purpose was: simply to put down on paper my experiences of living with cancer that other sufferers might have the courage to face what has to be faced. To know that hope walks with courage, to greet each new day with joy, and at the end of each day, to thank God for a bonus day—and for life itself.

Because of what it has taught me, I would not have changed my last quarter century, plus, for a fortune.

Amazing Grace.

If you enjoyed this book, please consider leaving a review on Amazon or Goodreads and helping more people to hear Mairi's story.

Other books from McGeary Media

Married to the Man Who Washed Himself Away—Joan Leech

All the Very Best!—Vin Garbutt

The Man Behind the Mask—John Anderson CBE

Printed in Great Britain
by Amazon

17731396R00058